KERMIT™
Music Manuscript Paper

32 Pages • 8½ x 8½ • 6 large size staves
Includes Music Notation Guide

WIDE STAFF

T0070552

HAL•LEONARD®

U.S. $7.99

ISBN 0-88188-506-1

MUSIC NOTATION GUIDE

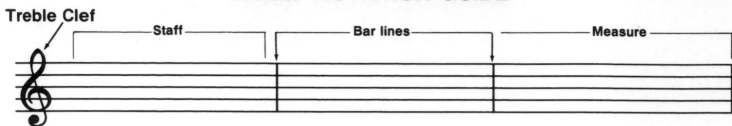

Treble Clef — Staff — Bar lines — Measure

Treble Clef — Lines & spaces

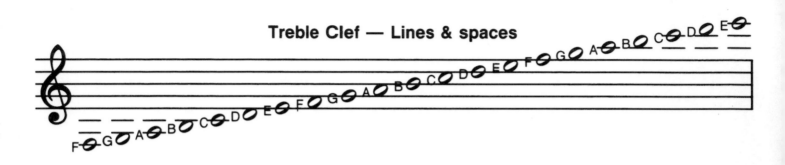

Bass Clef — Lines & spaces

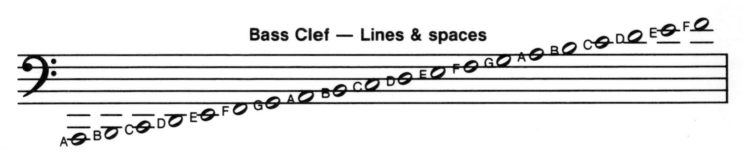

Time Signatures

4/4 4 beats per measure / A quarter note equals 1 beat	**3/4** 3 beats per measure / A quarter note equals 1 beat	**6/8** 6 beats per measure / An eighth note equals 1 beat

Notes & Rests

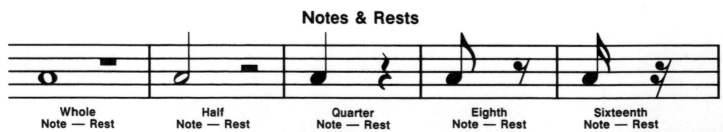

| Whole Note — Rest | Half Note — Rest | Quarter Note — Rest | Eighth Note — Rest | Sixteenth Note — Rest |

© 1986 HAL LEONARD PUBLISHING CORPORATION
International Copyright secured   All rights reserved.

Continued on back inside cove[r]

© 1986 Henson Associates, Inc.
HL00210013

© 1986 Henson Associates, Inc.
HL00210013

© 1986 Henson Associates, Inc.

HL00210013

© 1986 Henson Associates, Inc.

HL00210013

© 1986 Henson Associates, Inc.
HL00210013

© 1986 Henson Associates, Inc.
HL00210013

© 1986 Henson Associates, Inc.
HL00210013

© 1986 Henson Associates, Inc.
HL00210013

© 1986 Henson Associates, Inc.
HL00210013

© 1986 Henson Associates, Inc.
HL00210013

© 1986 Henson Associates, Inc.
HL00210013

© 1986 Henson Associates, Inc.
HL00210013

© 1986 Henson Associates, Inc.

HL00210013

© 1986 Henson Associates, Inc.
HL00210013

© 1986 Henson Associates, Inc.
HL00210013

© 1986 Henson Associates, Inc.
HL00210013

1986 Henson Associates, Inc.
L00210013

© 1986 Henson Associates, Inc.
HL00210013

1986 Henson Associates, Inc.
L00210013

© 1986 Henson Associates, Inc.
HL00210013

1986 Henson Associates, Inc.
L00210013

© 1986 Henson Associates, Inc.
HL00210013

© 1986 Henson Associates, Inc.
L00210013

© 1986 Henson Associates, Inc.
HL00210013

© 1986 Henson Associates, Inc.
HL00210013

© 1986 Henson Associates, Inc.
HL00210013

© 1986 Henson Associates, Inc.
HL00210013

© 1986 Henson Associates, Inc.
HL00210013

© 1986 Henson Associates, Inc.
HL00210013

© 1986 Henson Associates, Inc.
HL00210013

© 1986 Henson Associates, Inc.
HL00210013

© 1986 Henson Associates, Inc.
HL00210013

Key Signatures

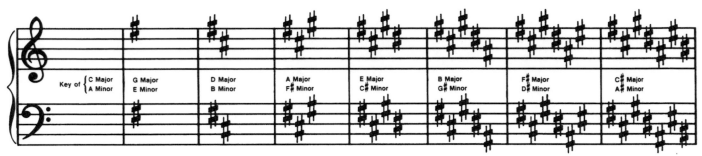

ORDER OF SHARPS: F - C - G - D - A - E - B

ORDER OF FLATS: B - E - A - D - G - C - F

Repeat Terms And Signs

D.C. al FINE Return to the beginning and play to Fine.

D.S. al FINE Return to 𝄋 and play to Fine.

D.C. al CODA Return to the beginning, play to ⊕ and skip to the Coda.

D.S. al CODA Return to 𝄋, play to ⊕ and skip to the Coda.

:‖ Return to the beginning or nearest ‖: and repeat.

Play through the first time, then skip to ⌐2 on the repeat.

Stems And Beams

Notes **below** the third line are written with stems **up**. Notes **on** or **above** the third line are written with stems down.

Stem direction of beamed notes or chords is determined by the note farthest from the third line.

HAL LEONARD
Manuscript Paper

A wide variety of manuscript paper available for your Keyboard and Guitar needs...

00210004...**Wide Staff Manuscript Paper (Red Cover)**; 32-page stitched book; large 6 staves per page; 8½″ x 8½″; Music Notation Guide.

00210001...**Standard Manuscript Paper (Yellow Cover)**; 64-page stitched book; 12 staves per page; 8½″ x 11″; punched to fit all ring binders; Music Notation Guide.

00210003...**Standard Loose Leaf Manuscript Paper (Pink Cover)**; 48 loose leaf pages; 12 staves per page printed both sides; 8½″ x 11″; punched to fit all ring binders; Music Notation Guide.

00210005...**Standard Wirebound Manuscript Paper (Green Cover)**; 96-page wirebound book; 12 staves per page; 8½″ x 11″; Music Notation Guide.

00210018...**Deluxe Wirebound Manuscript Paper (Rose Cover)**; 96-page wirebound book; **Premium paper**; 12 staves per page; 9″ x 12″; Music Notation Guide.

00210019...**Deluxe Wirebound Manuscript Paper (Gold Cover)**; 96-page wirebound book; **Premium paper**; 12 staves per page; 8½″ x 11″; Music Notation Guide.

00210006...**Wide Staff Wirebound Manuscript Paper (Aqua Cover)**; 32-page wirebound book; 6 staves per page; 8½″ x 8½″; Music Notation Guide.

00210002...**Deluxe Pad – 8½″ x 11″ Manuscript Paper (Blue Cover)**; Deluxe tear off pad with firm backing for easy writing; 32 sheets (64 pages) printed both sides; 12 staves per page; 8½″ x 11″; punched to fit all ring binders; Music Notation Guide.

00210000...**Deluxe Pad – 9″ x 12″ – Manuscript Paper (Taupe Cover)**; With firm backing for easy writing; 32 sheets (64 pages) printed both sides; 12 staves per page; 9″ x 12″; punched to fit all ring binders; Music Notation Guide.

00704357...**Guitar Manuscript Paper – Standard (Gold Cover)**; 64-page stitched book; 8½″ x 11″; 6-line staves on each page; 8 blank chord diagrams printed at bottom of each page; punched to fit all ring binders; Music Notation Guide.

00704350...**Guitar Manuscript Paper – Deluxe (Green Cover)**; Deluxe tear off pad with firm backing for easy writing; 32 sheets (64 pages); 5-line staves on each 9″ x 12″ page; 8 blank chord diagrams printed at the bottom of each page; punched to fit all ring binders; Music Notation Guide.

00704356...**Guitar Tablature Manuscript Paper – Standard (Tan Cover)**; 64-page stitched book; 8½″ x 11″; 6-line staves on each page; 8 blank chord diagrams printed at the bottom of each page; punched to fit all ring binders; Music Notation Guide.

00704355...**Guitar Tablature Manuscript Paper – Deluxe (Brown Cover)**; Deluxe tear off pad with firm backing for easy writing; 32 sheets (64 pages); 6-line staves on each 9″ x 12″ page; 8 blank chord diagrams printed at the bottom of each page; punched to fit all ring binders; Music Notation Guide.

00000023...**Garfield Manuscript Paper.** 9″ x 12″. Every page is perforated to tear out easily, and the paper is extremely durable. There's also a dictionary of musical terms, common musical notation, piano chord diagrams, a transposing chart and a circle of fifths.

00000034...**Garfield Manuscript Paper.** (9″ x 8″)

00210015...**Donald's Manuscript Paper**; 32-page stitched book with the Donald Duck character on each page; large 6-staves per page; 8½″ x 8½″; Music Notation Guide.

00210014...**Mickey's Manuscript Paper**; 32-page stitched book with the Mickey Mouse character on each page; large 6-staves per page; 8½″ x 8½″; Music Notation Guide.

00210012...**Miss Piggy Manuscript Paper**; 32-page stitched book with the Miss Piggy character on each page; large 6-staves per page; 8½″ x 8½″; Music Notation Guide.

00210013...**Kermit Music Manuscript Paper**; 32-page stitched book with the Kermit character on each page; large 6-staves per page; 8½″ x 8″½; Music Notation Guide.

00101787...**E-Z Play TODAY Manuscript Paper**; 48-page stitched; 6 staves per page; 9″ x 12″; punched to fit all ring binders; Music Notation Guide.

00243476...**EKM Manuscript Paper**; 48-page stitched; 6 staves per page; 6″ x 9″; Music Notation Guide.

Not all products are available outside the USA. 7/89

FOR MORE INFORMATION, SEE YOUR LOCAL MUSIC DEALER, OR WRITE TO:

HAL•LEONARD® CORPORATION

7777 W. BLUEMOUND RD. P.O. BOX 13819 MILWAUKEE, WI 53213

Distributed By
HAL LEONARD
ISBN-13: 978-0-88188-506-4

002100013